THE LIONS PART

the Lions part is an eclectic c̶o̶r̶
performers who collabo̶r̶
theatre pieces that transf̶e̶
as traditional theatres with
customs and heritage.

the Lions part's Bankside Fe̶s̶ _̶_̶u̶d̶ *Twelfth
Night*, are seasonal, theatre-ba̶ _̶s̶, springing from
time-honoured festivities and i̶t̶ ̶p̶lays, music and games in a
modern urban setting. The festivals reflect our interest in oral
history, the environment and local food.

the Lions part has toured nationally and worked in collaboration
with other arts organisations on celebrations and festivals
nationwide.

the Lions part company members

Callum Coates	Dorothy Lawrence
Rosalind Cressy	Tamsin Lewis
Sarah Finch	Kali Peacock
Duncan Law	Sonia Ritter
Company Manager	Emma Butler Smith

FRESH GLORY PRODUCTIONS

Fresh Glory Productions is a theatrical producing company based
in London, producing their own shows as well as co-productions
with existing theatre companies.

Recent work includes: *Huck* (with Shapeshifter and the Theatre
Chipping Norton, UK and Ireland tour); *Up the Duff* (with York
Theatre Royal); *Frozen* by Bryony Lavery (UK tour); *The City
Wives' Confederacy* (with the Lions part, Greenwich Playhouse);
and *Play* (with the Theatre Chipping Norton and Latitude Festival).

Executive Producer	Rosalind Riley
Associate Producers	Emma Butler Smith
	Dorothy Lawrence
Production Assistant	Lee Henderson

Sarah Finch, Dorothy Lawrence, Kali Peacock,
Sonia Ritter, Natasha Tamar
and the Lions part

LILIES
ON THE LAND

NICK HERN BOOKS
London
www.nickhernbooks.co.uk

A Nick Hern Book

Lilies on the Land first published in Great Britain as a paperback original in 2010 by Nick Hern Books Limited, The Glasshouse, 49a Goldhawk Road, London W12 8QP

Reprinted 2011 (twice), 2012

Lilies on the Land copyright © 2010 Sarah Finch, Dorothy Lawrence, Kali Peacock, Sonia Ritter, Natasha Tamar and the Lions part

Front cover photograph by Neil Smith
Cover image designed by Dewynters
Cover designed by Ned Hoste, 2H

Typeset by Nick Hern Books, London
Printed in Great Britain by Mimeo Ltd, Huntingdon, Cambridgeshire PE29 6XX

A CIP catalogue record for this book is available from the British Library

ISBN   978 1 84842 113 4

Introduction

In 2001, the Lions part decided to stage Christopher Fry's play, *A Sleep of Prisoners*, which explores the troubled minds of four soldiers held prisoners of war. As a companion piece, we wanted to stage a sister play: a play that gave a voice to the wartime experiences of women. The subject of the Women's Land Army had come up after reading poems by Land Girls (mostly unknown) in an obscure book of war poems. We later found many of them came from *The Land Girl*, a contemporary journal published in the 1940s and written and read by the women themselves.* We began to realise that we knew little about the extraordinary role the Women's Land Army played in World War II: certainly a Forgotten Army.

the Lions part company members are experienced in devising theatre and we were keen to develop a new play. We decided to go (as no doubt most of the Land Girls would say), to the 'horse's mouth'. We wrote an open letter to *Saga Magazine* asking ex-Women's Land Army members if they would consider sending us any material relating to their experience in the Land Army, that might help us to create a play.

We expected only a small number of replies, but the response was staggering. Almost one hundred and fifty letters flowed in from women from all walks of life; memories and recollections, anecdotes, poems, photos, newspaper cuttings and wartime memorabilia. It took over three days to go through all the letters: we read out loud what we could to each other. What resonated most was the breadth of the human experience and the depth of each individual woman's feelings. Most movingly, memories that were highly personal to each writer also seemed to be part of one collective voice, one extraordinary shared experience, full of strength, courage and love. This in essence, straight from the horse's mouth, became the heart of *Lilies on the Land*.

---

* We were also sent copies by ex-Women's Land Army members: many were gathered and published by Vita Sackville-West in *The Women's Land Army* (1944 Michael Joseph Ltd), republished with additions in 1977 by the Imperial War Museum.

The rehearsal room filled up with pieces of paper and pictures: charts and diagrams, cut-and-pasted lists of full-length recollections, anecdotes, poems, sayings, songs. The floor, table and chairs were covered. Slowly key elements of content began to emerge and take form. We were swiftly learning the farming year. It was essential to grasp the exacting labour demanded of the women, physically and mentally. Certain elements became key – signing up, weather, particular farming skills, animals, dances, soldiers, those left at home, POWs, food, love – and death.

We arranged to meet many of the women who had written to us; we heard yet more stories, told with wonderful animation and vivacity. And some of these women became the chief inspiration of the four principal characters created by the four actors in the company.

A timeline and pattern began to emerge. One seasonal turn of the year and its accompanying tasks swung through the duration of the play. Woven into it were momentous events of a longer duration: the War from 1939 to 1945.

Once we had a script to rehearse with, a distinct playing style began to emerge. The play unfolded 'out front' to the audience and the narrative was carried along by the shared enactment of each event as it happened, in that moment in the past. Faith in living history, as well as the spirit and dynamism of the people to whom the events actually occurred, lifted the page onto the stage with vigour. The playing could be fresh, open and immediate, the flow of the play driven by each character and their immediate circumstances. One quality stood out: each Land Girl sustains her own unique and independent journey even as events and experiences are communally recalled and shared.

With Arts Council support, *Lilies on the Land* toured outer-London churches in 2001. In 2003, the Lions part took to the road nationally and played to ninety-seven per cent audience capacity, among whom were many ex-Land Girls and their families.

Through careful amendment and reworking, the play has evolved and grown, but sustains its original form and content. It is most exciting to see *Lilies on the Land* in London's West End; a living testament to a generation of truly remarkable women.

Staging and Performing *Lilies on the Land*

The nature of time in *Lilies on the Land* is fundamental to its dramatic power. The fabric of the play is made up of memories that happen in 'real time', they are not reflective. When we heard ex-Women's Land Army members telling us their stories, they relived the experiences they recalled and it made them buzz with excitement. In playing therefore, *Lilies on the Land* realises each story physically and emotionally in the moment it is told, not as something that is being recalled with nostalgia.

Whilst the inspiration that fires the women to speak, sparks from Sir Winston Churchill's death, and the era they recall is some twenty-five years before, the dynamic of the telling is in the present, to a twenty-first-century audience. Some of the women we met were in their late eighties. It is essential, therefore, to avoid generalised nostalgia if the audience are to live along with the women as they relive their experiences. The three timelines co-exist and move together, creating the shape of the theatrical experience: January 1965, 1939–45, and now.

In considering the staging, there are two other principal characters in *Lilies on the Land*: World War II and the land itself, both surrounding and underpinning all that happens to the women. The enormity of the war and its place in history carries huge weight, so does not require undue additional theatrical emphasis. The land perhaps, in this day and age, may require more thought to bring it alive in the theatre. The weather is another major element in the play, an intrinsic part of any recollection of working on the land. All three are, of course, rich subjects for inspiring stage design, sound, and lighting.

As with many epic subjects, simplicity and minimalism can work amazingly well: trusting what an audience brings to the depiction of such subjects, as well as the clarity with which they are described by the characters.

Doubling

We have indicated particular Land Girls for some doublings. These are based on the qualities of the cast of this production and work well. Other characters we have left unspecified, to indicate freedom of choice – which we ourselves have used with different casts.

Although we have always performed *Lilies* with four actors, the play is wonderfully versatile and the cast could easily be expanded for a larger company. The doubling can vary and as long as the story is told clearly, it matters little which actor takes on the other characters. Any doubling is possible and depends more on the ability of different cast members to take on accents and characterisation rather than adhering rigidly to any suggestions here.

Whatever a company decides to do, it is essential that the four Land Girls are four individual actors and that the story they are telling is the focus of the stage at any given point.

Sound Effects

The BBC holds extensive archive recordings from the BBC Radio broadcasts of Sir Winston Churchill's funeral and throughout World War II. These can be listened to at the British Library Sound Archive.

the Lions part
2010

This version of *Lilies on the Land* was performed at the Arts Theatre, London, on 8 June 2010, with the following cast:

MARGIE	Dorothy Lawrence
PEGGY	Kali Peacock
POPPY	Sarah Finch
VERA	Rosalind Cressy

Directed by Sonia Ritter
Set design by Jane Linz Roberts
Lighting design by Michael Scott
Sound and music by Peter Readman
Costume by Constance Mackenzie
Original music sourced and arranged by Tamsin Lewis
Produced by Fresh Glory Productions

In previous productions (2001, 2003, 2005), the role of *Vera* was played by Natasha Tamar, Sonia Ritter and Caroline Lonq.

Characters

MARGIE

Margie is from Newcastle. She refers to herself as a townie. She is very naive and childlike – though not childish. Appearance-wise, Margie describes herself as being very pretty, with masses of curls and looking very 'doll-like' in her uniform, with a liking for make-up and curlers. She is warm and constantly in a state of surprise. She ends up in a farm on her own and has a difficult time. She spends a lot of time alone and this leads her to become more introspective as the play progresses. She is funny and affectionate. When I met the real Margie she was in her late seventies. What struck me was that her childlike, open nature and her energy and enthusiasm seemed to be unchanged by age and experience. She would need to have a County Durham or Newcastle accent. She is brought up a Methodist and is from quite a big family.

PEGGY

Peggy is a happy, confident young cockney from a large East End family – that is, until she finds herself in the middle of the country, not knowing 'one end of a cow from the other'. Keen to do her bit for the War Effort and not afraid to roll up her sleeves and get stuck in, Peg maintains her sense of humour and her positive attitude... most of the time. During her time in the Land Army, Peggy grows up pretty quickly; she enjoys the work, revels in the camaraderie of the other girls, but also loves being out on her own in the fields on her tractor – her ploughing skills are second to none! Taking each day as it comes, the last thing she expects is to fall in love... both with the countryside and with the Jim the Foreman! Peggy is a mixture of two incredible women who describe their journey in the Women's Land Army as the best of times and the worst of times – but are adamant that they wouldn't change a thing.

POPPY

Poppy is from Oxfordshire, brought up in a happy and privileged family, and used to a comfortable lifestyle. Her family assumes, at the outbreak of war, that she would join the Wrens, but the romantic posters enticed her into signing up for the WLA. The tough life on the land is a shock, but she is ready to learn, and throws herself into it all with energy and enthusiasm, finding the strength and the resources within herself to cope. A confident and outgoing person, she enjoys dances and romance and, eventually, life on the land. Her accent is RP, but without affectation. Poppy is the nickname given to her by the farmhands, once she has proved she can become one of them! Both of the Land Girls who were most influential in the creation of Poppy had a zest for life, and an ability to look for the good in everything.

VERA

Vera is a rather complex character who responds very thoughtfully to the things that happen to her. She asks questions and expects to make her own way, likes to muck in and yet isn't really 'one of the girls'. She's educated, and frustrated with old-fashioned views of women. The war is an opportunity for her, in a way – partly to get away from her snobby stepmother and partly to go out into the world and find out who she really is. Perhaps she'll never be satisfied with life, but perhaps she'll make a difference to others along the way. Competent and hearty, she is in some ways the most lonely of the four Land Girls, and probably the only one who's read Virginia Woolf…

The four girls also play the following roles, though it is also possible to perform the play with a larger cast.

INTERVIEW LADY
MR BAINBRIDGE
MRS BAINBRIDGE
STATIONMASTER
TINY LADY
GIRL
DON
FARMER
ALFRED
JOYCE
ROSE
JIM
SOLDIER
ANNOUNCER
MRS BOTTOMLY
GRANDFATHER
LADY FARMER
ITALIAN
FARMER
ANNIE
GLIDER-FACTORY MEN
SERVICE FARMER
FOREMAN
AMERICAN
MATRON
CONSCIENTIOUS OBJECTOR
OLD GEORGE
VICAR

This text went to press before the end of rehearsals and so may differ slightly from the play as performed.

ACT ONE

1939–1942

It is now Sunday 24th January 1965. The play moves to autumn 1939, as the women recall when they joined the Women's Land Army.

Radio playing BBC Home Service.

MARGIE: *In a bedroom, rollers in her hair, dress on, applying her make-up at the mirror.*

PEGGY: *In a farmhouse kitchen, in an apron, at a table, preparing lunch for the family.*

POPPY: *In a drawing room, wearing her coat, ready to go to church, with flowers.*

VERA: *In the kitchen/diner of a small flat, wearing a robe, with a coffee, about to start typing.*

It is 8 a.m. The BBC announces Winston Churchill's death.

POPPY. He's gone –

PEGGY. Shush –

MARGIE. The old bugger –

VERA. He *jilted* us –

  Radio comes up and fades out.

PEGGY. Well I'm blowed… (*Calls.*) Jim…

POPPY. So many… so many…

MARGIE. Oh my God… I'm going to be late…

VERA. He *jilted* us.

  The radio continues with Churchill's speech.

CHURCHILL'S VOICE. We shall go on to the end, we shall
    fight in France,
    We shall fight on the seas and oceans,
    We shall fight with growing confidence and growing strength
    in the air, we shall defend our island, whatever the cost may
    be,
    We shall fight on the beaches,
    We shall fight on the landing grounds,
    We shall fight in the fields and in the streets,
    We shall fight in the hills.
    We shall never surrender, and even if, which I do not for a
    moment believe, this island or a large part of it were
    subjugated and starving, then our Empire beyond the seas,
    armed and guarded by the British Fleet, would carry on the
    struggle, until, in God's good time, the new world, with all
    its power and might, steps forth to the rescue and the
    liberation of the old.

The radio broadcast fades and ends under the WOMEN*'s
voices.*

MARGIE. Eee, that darned poster.

VERA. Jumper and breeches.

PEGGY. 'Lend a Hand on the Land.'

POPPY. A girl, head held high, golden hair, smiling and
    proud...

PEGGY. On a hayrick.

POPPY. That's what started it for me.

MARGIE. In me mind's eye, I saw before us green fields...

PEGGY. Crops of vegetables.

POPPY. Perhaps flowers.

MARGIE. All things bright and beautiful.

VERA. Girls in green and beige...

VERA *and* MARGIE. Their faces and arms...

VERA, MARGIE *and* PEGGY. Tanned…

ALL. Hair flowing in the breeze…

POPPY. And wielding a pitchfork! My mother wanted me to join the WRNS: elegant and sophisticated; admirals and their wives were all prepared to pull appropriate strings.

VERA. 'Dig for Victory.'

PEGGY. 'Your Country Needs You…'

MARGIE. The Army and all of them were in Newcastle at the time. You couldn't see anything for uniforms

POPPY. Men in uniform.

MARGIE. And I *wanted* one.

PEGGY. I had the choice of domestic work in hospitals, the NAAFI, or the Women's Land Army. Well hospitals was out cos I was a bit squeamish, and the NAAFI, well, my mother vetoed that. 'You'll be serving strong drink to men over the counter, over my dead body.' So that left the Land Army… 'A nice healthy outdoor occupation for a lass.' But I didn't know one end of a cow from the other.

VERA. Well, I'd just been to college and I worked in a bank, a reserved profession. I wasn't allowed to wear trousers and I loved the look of the breeches. So I thought, well maybe, I'll join the Land Army, do something for the War Effort. When I talked to my boss, he was very unpleasant about it, he said I was making things difficult for him. My stepmother was horrified: 'You're wasting your education. You'll soon be bored working with yokels who are wood from the neck up.' The next day, I went and signed up.

MARGIE. I wrote to the Ministry of Agriculture and Fisheries for the necessary forms. I found a lot of questions to be answered…

QUESTION ONE (POPPY). What type of land work would you like to do?

MARGIE. I put Market Gardening and Horticulture.

QUESTION TWO (VERA). Which part of Britain would you prefer?

MARGIE. I put the South of England, thinking that most of the fruit and veg was grown there.

QUESTION THREE (PEGGY). Would you care to be privately billeted or hostel billeted?

MARGIE. I put hostel billeted, as I thought it would be nicer to work along with other girls and have the company. However, they didn't take any notice of my replies and I was recruited out to a 'private farm' in Murphy Tyers, Murphy Hill, outside Darlington.

PEGGY. I was surprised to find I had to go to Oxford Street for my interview. I stood in front of this lady, with what I call a five-pound-note voice. She twirled a gold pencil continuously in her long fingers, as she fired a barrage of questions at me:

INTERVIEW LADY. 'Do you think it's all going to be feeding chickens with lovely weather?'

PEGGY. 'I have been hop-picking, you know, since the age of three.' Well, she jumped back as if I had fleas.

POPPY. For my interview, I was wearing a stylish new cotton frock that my aunt had made for me. It had a red-and-black pleated skirt and a splash of poppies on the bodice, I borrowed my friend's high-heeled sandals, and to complete the picture, my hair was piled on top with two ringlets hanging over my forehead – which was, after all, the fashion and it looked great on Veronica Lake. My gaze went to the poster. The Land Girl was smiling, as though advertising toothpaste, and... dressed in a uniform. 'Am I prepared to swap my dress style for that?'

MARGIE. When I got home from work one day, there was me uniform. 'Parcel upstairs for you, Marge.' Pop had put it on the bed for us.

ALL. Two green jumpers.

Two pairs of breeches.

VERA. (Good.)

ALL. Two overall coats.

POPPY. (In light khaki.)

ALL. Two pairs of dungarees.

Six pairs of long socks.

PEGGY. (Woollen.)

ALL. Three Aertex shirts.

VERA. (Shapeless.)

ALL. One pair of ankle boots –

POPPY. (Those boots, Mummy wept when she saw them.)

ALL. One pair of shoes.

One pair of gumboots.

POPPY. (Wellingtons.)

MARGIE. (For when it's wet.)

ALL. One hat.

MARGIE. (Gorgeous.)

ALL. One green tie.

One overcoat.

VERA. (Not actually issued until 1943.)

ALL. One mackintosh.

MARGIE. (Down to your ankles.)

ALL. Two towels.

One oilskin sou'wester.

One red armlet… and a metal badge.

MARGIE. The signing-up certificate said:

VERA. 'You have made your home fields –

PEGGY....your battlefield.'

The WOMEN *reveal Land Army uniforms under their clothes. This may be done in silence or during the dialogue. Throughout the next speech a song is quietly sung, perhaps one of those from the play repertoire or a well-known song from the war years, like 'Wish Me Luck as You Wave Me Goodbye'.*

Every time I think of that day I chuckle to myself. The uniforms came in standard sizes. The breeches were supposed to reach just below the knee, but mine came down to my calves and bulged beneath my knee-length socks. The heavy brogue shoes I could hardly lift off the ground. You can imagine how I looked. Wish me luck.

MARGIE. It bucketed down the day I travelled to Murphy Tyers. Me mam took me. There I was, all in me uniform. We got a train into Darlington and Mam hired a taxi and he took us to Murphy Hill. I'd never seen anything like it; the driveway was all muck and plother, potholes full of water. When I got out in the stackyard, it was bucketing. I bent down to pick me cases up. Taxi man had just thrown them out, got back in and he was away before I could even say goodbye to me mam. They're off, and I'm standing there wondering where I was. Me hat looked like a wet lettuce. Then I saw this figure standing in the doorway doing this... (*Beckoning with finger.*)

MR BAINBRIDGE. Look what they've sent us, she'd make a good ornament for t'mantelpiece.

MARGIE. I splodged towards the door and went in.

POPPY. My mother saw me off on the Watlington Donkey from Prince's Risborough to Lewknor Holt, having first seated me safely beside two elderly ladies, headed for the same destination. The train only had one carriage, at the station they had to bring steps for people to alight. The train was to arrive at four seventeen.

VERA. My calling-up papers arrived, number –

The numbers overlap each other.

10873.

POPPY. 148785.

MARGIE. 26538.

PEGGY. 0101337.

VERA. And my travel warrants and instructions. I caught the quarter past nine train to Manchester and then the slow train through Wigan, and got off at somewhere called Hoscar, miles from anywhere. There was nobody to meet me, no taxi, no one. I just stood there. It got dark.

STATIONMASTER. Well, what are you still standing there for?

VERA. It was the stationmaster. I explained to him what had happened.

STATIONMASTER. You can borrow my bike. I'll walk home.

VERA. I'd never ridden a bicycle before.

STATIONMASTER. Now, you can't get lost, you just keep going down that road till you get there... it's only about six miles.

VERA. So I did.

PEGGY. I was immediately sent on a tractor-driving course at High Halden, Kent. It was brilliant, we were taught the rudiments of ploughing and other field work, and how to back a four-wheeled wagon – difficult until you get the hang of it. I missed home.

VERA. This tiny lady opened the door and looked me up and down and said

TINY LADY. I'm only allowing you in the house once with those shoes on, my Earnest has to peg them up in the shed and you'll do the same thing.

VERA. So I stepped in carefully onto the very shiny lino, and the next thing I saw was this dog wearing knitted booties.

POPPY. I thought all houses in the British Isles had flush lavatories... an old earth closet way down the garden path... no bathroom, only a sink and an old pump in the kitchen. What had I done? My visions of tossing hay in the summer sun faded...

VOICE. Report to the cow stable at six thirty.

POPPY. A time of day that had never previously existed for me. A candle to light me to my bed... September... Cold lino, marble-topped washstand, flowery-patterned jug and bowl – the matching potty under the bed. I climbed into bed, clinging to the hope that the war would be over in the morning. Six o'clock arrived – the war was still on... a quick cup of tea... out to the cow stable: a long building, lit by a hurricane lamp, where about twenty cows were tied, I found the smell revolting.

MARGIE. Mr Bainbridge, the farmer, called me down. I said, 'It's still bedtime!'

MR BAINBRIDGE. Come on, get thee selv' up!

MARGIE. So I came down. No tea or anything, she was still in bed. He gave me a bucket, he had a bucket and he took me to this great big long shed. So we got to the first cow and he sits down like this and he had his cap and he turned it round that way. Then he put his head on the side of the cow, bucket between his knees, here, got hold of the cow's underneath and started doing this. (*She demonstrates milking.*) 'Eee!' I said, 'I thought that come out of bottles in the shops.'

MR BAINBRIDGE (*laughs*). Well then, thou's got a lot to learn. Come on, have a try.

MARGIE. He watched me sit down.

MR BAINBRIDGE. Go on, lass, get hold of her tits.

MARGIE. Well, I was so embarrassed – I thought, what a rude man! Pop had taken me to see the pantomime in Newcastle and everyone had laughed when Idle Jack in *Jack and the Beanstalk* had tried to milk the cow by pumping its tail up and down! I thought, sitting there, that it wasn't funny at all – it was just a jolly good idea. I hadn't really taken in what he'd showed us. Had he taken the cows two back things first? I just didn't like to use that rude word – not even to meself. Then again, he could have taken her two front things first. Would the cow know and object if I took her things in the wrong order? Perhaps it was one thing from the front and another thing from the back. The possibilities seemed endless. Was it rather like bell-ringing? If you didn't get it right the first time round, the whole thing fell apart. The cow was still munching away at her food and it seemed the most sensible thing to do was to get the job over with before she realised what was happening at the other end! So I got down, put the bucket between my knees here, took one thing in each hand and squeezed. Well, I couldn't get this milk out! I got two drops out in about an hour and a half. Not even enough to make a cup of tea.

VERA. A group of us were dumped in a field for potato lifting. The tractor turned the soil ahead of us and we were stretched along the field with bent-over backs, arms caked in wet soil up to the elbows. After about two rows, my back broke in two places. And all this while, Mrs Knitted-Booties-Hitler sat in her car at the end of the field to ensure we weren't having a second's rest.

PEGGY. Guns started firing.

All the LAND GIRLS *react as if a bomb has fallen*

I heard the whizz of a shell, I ran out to the garden.

GIRL. Get in!

PEGGY. I went down the shelter –

DON. It's all right, it's only the Germans dropping bombs.

POPPY. The farmer told us to go and feed the calves. I thought I'd take a short cut across the yard, it was only a few steps and it was muck and I wondered why the others were going round the side. I stepped out into the yard and started to sink, I went in, and in, and in, right up to my armpits – they had to get a pitchfork to haul me out. I lost my wellingtons and my socks. They had to hose me down.

VERA. Mrs Hitler kept pigs, and I was sent to clean them out. The pigs were being fed kale – long thick stalks. The pigs ate the leaves, chewed the stalks, and then trampled them into all that sort of sloppy pig muck. I had to get the stalks out of the sties and onto the muck-hill, but I couldn't balance them on my shovel and if I pierced them with a fork they wouldn't come off, and it seemed the only way to deal with these stalks was to manhandle them; so I picked them up out of that sloppy pig muck, and carried them one by one down the passage and flung them onto the muck-hill. The mess I was in was unbelievable. The little pigs kept running between my legs. My nice new dungarees were absolutely stiff with a mixture of cow muck and pig muck and swill.

MARGIE. Mr Bainbridge took me up to this field and he told me to start luking. 'Eee,' I said. 'Isn't it nice.' It was a lovely September day, the sun was shining, birds were singing, there were the trees and the hills, and the village in the distance. 'Ah,' I said. 'It's a nice view.'

MR BAINBRIDGE. Hast th' finished?

MARGIE. Yes.

MR BAINBRIDGE. Good, cos now tha's seen it, you won't need to look again. Dost thou see them in the grass?

MARGIE. It was covered – nettles, dockings, thistles up to me waist. He bent down, took out his knife and started cutting them.

MR BAINBRIDGE. Now, that's what we call luking.

MARGIE. And he gave me a hand sickle.

MR BAINBRIDGE. And you better get on with it.

MARGIE. By meself? It was a five-acre field. It took me three weeks.

PEGGY. I'd drive around the farms on small Fordson tractors or five-gear John Deeres, and I'd think, 'I'm working, I'm working for the War Effort.'

POPPY. I was told to clean up after a cow had calved, I felt ill as *it* kept sliding back through the prongs into the gutter. The farmhands were hysterical with laughter, I was just hysterical.

PEGGY. One farm, the men chicken-wired us in round some hayricks, and there were all these rats, rats falling on us, rats scurrying around us, and then they put the dogs in to kill the rats and they all stood outside and watched us, farm workers on the farm, not one of us flinched.

Slowly, the LAND GIRLS *begin to sing 'Lily's on the Land' by Ralph Butler and Tolchard Evans.*

POPPY. We never knew what we would be doing.

PEGGY. Cleaning out pigsties while holding your breath, then diving outside to gulp fresh air –

VERA. Carting bales of straw –

MARGIE. Milking –

PEGGY. Agony for the wrists, you have to overcome the swelling.

POPPY. My hands were so stiff, in the morning I couldn't turn the alarm clock off.

VERA. One girl had to dig a grave for a horse, and the farmer cut chunks off it to feed the dogs while she was digging.

PEGGY. Muck-spreading with pig dung –

POPPY. A cold miserable job –

VERA. Drenching October rain –

PEGGY. Trouser legs wet through –

MARGIE. Army boots sodden –

POPPY. Those boots, they blistered my feet.

VERA. Wet through to your vest –

MARGIE. Grading seed potatoes, in the dry –

POPPY. Eight-stone sacks of potatoes are heavy to move –

VERA. Nights drawing in –

MARGIE. Clocks change –

PEGGY. When we get home there's a first-come line to dry
your breeches at the fire in the hall. Not much chance with
fifty girls and a fireguard.

VERA. Six a.m., breeches and boots back on, still feeling
damp.

POPPY. Not a pleasant experience.

MARGIE. Bringing in drinking water, hand pumped from a
landmine crater in the middle of a meadow.

PEGGY. Carting –

POPPY. Calving –

VERA. Clearing fields –

PEGGY. Apple-picking –

VERA. More spud-lifting and –

ALL. Threshing.

PEGGY. The threshing machine's worked by an old steam
engine, which belches out disgusting smoke. When moving
it from farm to farm – metal cleats have to be removed from
the wheels and bolted on again by us girls – hard on the
hands.

POPPY. One girl has to climb onto the stack and throw sheaves
onto the machine with a pitchfork.

PEGGY. Another girl stands in a sort of well next to a drum, with a knife attached to her wrist with a strap, she's called the band-cutter.

VERA. The feeder catches the stook and the band-cutter slides the knife in flat, and flicks it back to cut the string, grabs the string by the knot.

ALL. You never wasted string.

PEGGY. The feeder then fans the sheaf out onto the drum, which moves along a canvas belt.

POPPY. The threshed corn comes out at the other end to be poured into sacks and loaded onto a cart.

MARGIE. Seven lads arrived with their gripes and their forks. I was put at the chaff end, to guide the dusty chaff into sacks, tie them up and replace them for the next lot.

PEGGY. The dirt gets right into your eyelids, your lashes and your hair –

MARGIE *sneezes*.

ALL. Bless you.

MARGIE. You've never heard such a noise –

ALL. Whirring, wheezing, rattling.

They repeat these words between them to create the noise of the threshing machine.

PEGGY. Look at us – the Golden-Green-All-Girl Threshing Gang.

VERA. My hair went grey –

POPPY. We wore turbans.

MARGIE. But it was a barley day, wasn't it! Barley's full of ears, sharp and spiky. I only had me best green jumper on, khaki socks and me hair all curly – I wanted to look posh, cos I never got out or saw anybody and there were all these lads. Well, I was covered in barley horns, the back of me jumper, I looked like a porcupine.

VERA. This girl Anna and me took turns as band-cutter and feeder. We got out of rhythm once, and instead of cutting the string I got Anna's fingers...

POPPY. A man handed me a stick...

VOICE. That's to kill the rats with...

PEGGY. As the sheaves were raised up high, mice would often fall out of them. They'd be ignored and would scamper off to freedom, but one of the girls below was on the receiving end once – a mouse fell into her open-necked shirt and got trapped in her cleavage. Brave man, I think his name was Mr Willis, quick as a flash, thrust his large hand into the forbidden territory and extracted the mouse. What a stroke of luck for him! 'Please God, send another mouse and I'll be ready,' but the silent prayer from all the rest of the men... remained unanswered.

POPPY. Dick, the Foreman, told the farmhands that I was gentry and they were to call me Miss Houghton. Then they tried it on, offering me a pail of bull's milk – now they call me Poppy.

VERA. We caught mice of roughly the same size and saved them in our pockets, till lunchtime. We took them over to the road, lined them up by their tails, and raced them across it. No cars – no petrol.

POPPY. To stop the mice running up our legs, we copied the farmhands and tied string around each leg. We started a new female fashion.

PEGGY. The attraction of hedging and ditching... was the fire.

POPPY. Lovely to sit by at lunchtime.

VERA. If we were near a farm or a cottage, we asked for water to make tea. We had this huge black pot which we balanced on the fire, and into it we dropped a handful of tea and let it boil. Then we dipped our mugs in, took as much as we wanted, and oh how good that tastes!

MARGIE. Lunch in a haversack.

PEGGY. A tin box.

POPPY. Greaseproof paper.

POPPY *and* PEGGY. One cheese sandwich, one jam sandwich and an apple.

PEGGY. I still to this day can't eat a cheese sandwich.

VERA. Slices of bread with some kind of paste on them...
We're supposed to get double cheese rations.

MARGIE. 'Ere, have mine.

POPPY. Fresh bread.

PEGGY. Cold milk straight from the cooler, fattening but healthy.

MARGIE. Slices of boiled beetroot in white bread – pink pieces.

POPPY. On special occasions, we have a slice of sponge cake made with liquid paraffin.

VERA. Half an hour for lunch with thick original –

ALL. – margarine sandwiches

The following two stories could be intertwined, they are relaxed anecdotes.

PEGGY. We were sitting eating our sandwiches on top of a fence, which surrounded a stockyard full of cattle. As one moved within our reach, blonde bombshell, Gladys, scratched his head and his back. As he didn't move but kept chewing the cud, Glad suddenly decides to sit on him. Well, with a snort he took off, and the rest of the stock started after him. Fortunately they were too crowded to do anything but pound round the outside of the field – so they had to come past us again. We all leaned forward and grabbed Glad and then all of us fell backwards off the fence. 'Course, she could've easily been killed.

POPPY. I was soaking wet. The farmer said, 'Go to my wife and she'll give you something to wear.' She was a massive great woman – she gave me this brassiere – you could have used it for a hammock.

The GIRLS *sing 'Don't Fence Me In' by Robert Fletcher and Cole Porter. The* GIRLS *enjoy acting out the Wild West.*

As the farmhouse was too far away, there was the question of where we would go to spend a penny. The farmhands jumped over the hedge.

JOYCE (MARGIE). Taking a 'hedge ticket'.

POPPY. We held a discussion on this, I lost the toss and was nominated to approach the farmer. 'We need a proper lavatory.' He went purple with rage. I thought he was going to blow a gasket.

FARMER. Git back and pick them tatters.

POPPY. No, I will not.

ALFRED (PEGGY). 'Fraid yer might get stung on nettles, hee, hee?

POPPY. Said Alfred. I said, 'If that is your answer to our request, you can pick your own potatoes.' I turned my back to walk away.

FARMER. Come back 'ere, miss, yer can 'ave yer toilet, where would yer like it put?

POPPY. Leading the farmhands round the back of the lorry, he gave them each a spade and told them to dig a hole at the end of the field. I was getting to the end of my row of potatoes when the farmer came over...

FARMER. We've finished the toilet, go and sees if ye like it.

POPPY. I walked towards it, sensing, without looking back, that they were all waiting for my approval. Attached to the front, tied on securely with string was a large piece of cardboard and in red paint: 'LADIES ONLY'. Lifting the tarpaulin flap, I went in. A gaping black hole with wooden handrails on either side – presumably to hold on to with legs astride! What would happen when your dungarees were round your ankles and you lost balance? I beckoned the girls to come over. Joyce said...

JOYCE (MARGIE). I'd rather go over the hedge.

POPPY. So I went back to the farmer and said we all appreciated what he and his men had done for us, but please could we have some wooden planks across the hole, just in case we were unfortunate enough to slip in. He complied. We got our lav.

PEGGY. I wee'd on a rabbit once. I don't know who was more frightened – me or the rabbit. I know I was the one running down the hill with me dungarees round me ankles.

They sing 'Run Rabbit, Run Rabbit' by Noel Gay and Ralph Butler.

From the radio, a BBC Home Service broadcast: London Blitz, 1940.

MARGIE. Brass-monkey weather – we worked outside whatever it was doing.

VERA. If it was wet, you put a hessian sack over your head and one round your waist; it was warmer and drier than the issue macs.

POPPY. Carrying sacks of potatoes on our shoulders.

PEGGY. I was sent to a hostel in the Midlands. We stayed at the old vicarage. It was lovely.

VERA. Rose dumped her sack and said the farmer could

ROSE (POPPY). Stick 'is potatoes up his Khyber Pass, 'er was back off to Brum.

PEGGY. There were three great big bedrooms with bunk beds called the Peach, Pink and Blue Dormitories and an attic upstairs, which me and five other girls lived in. I named it Heaven.

MARGIE. Hands so cold you'd cut yourself and not notice till your hands warmed up again.

VERA. It was a relief to go and milk the cows. We put our hands up between their udders and their legs to keep them warm. The cows didn't seem to mind.

PEGGY. Being in large dormitories bothered some of the girls, but being one of seven, I felt quite at home and we all got on together... eventually.

MARGIE. Frost round our heads and our hats.

VERA. Swilling out the midden.

PEGGY. Ploughing.

MARGIE. Driving a tractor.

ALL. Ploughing.

PEGGY. There's a satisfaction that goes with ploughing –

VERA. Watching the way the ribbon of furrow is flung unbroken on its back.

POPPY. When the gulls are inland, they swoop in formation, eager for the freshly turned furrow.

MARGIE. It was a foggy, frosty day. Stan, the farmhand gave me the orders to work on a tractor, coupled to a disc harrow, ready to plough a fifty-acre field, then he was off before I had a chance to explain to him that I had never driven anything in me life, let alone a tractor! I did as I was bid, ploughing the whole afternoon, never able to stop – because he had never shown me how. When the field was finished – in record time – I had to drive the tractor right into the farmyard, praying there would be somebody there to stop the darned thing! Thankfully, Stan saw me coming and jumped on board and turned the engine off. Mr Bainbridge was so amazed with my work that he gave me butter and cheese to send home to me mam. He never did know the truth.

PEGGY. I'd been taught to plough around the field's perimeter first, about ten feet from the edge. This forms the headland

and is the last bit to be ploughed, going round in a circle when the field itself has been ploughed in lovely straight furrows. I'm short-sighted and need glasses to see distances. So I put them on, put in my line marker – that's a wooden stake with a scarf tied to the top – turned the tractor towards it and started ploughing. It was going really well. Jim, the Foreman, came by and said –

JIM. Well done, you have made a really good job, I'll bring the manager round this afternoon so he can see how well you're doing.

PEGGY. Being a bit vain – I had of course put my glasses in my pocket as soon as I'd spotted him. I rather liked the look of him and he seemed to like me, so I didn't want him to see me in me glasses.

As I was lining up the tractor to start the first furrow of the new section – I spotted Jim and the manager on the other side of the field. I whipped off my glasses and turned the tractor. Now, come on, Peg, all you need to do to get a really nice straight furrow is keep the stake in line with the bonnet of the tractor. This I did and both Jim and the manager stood on the other side of the field and watched me. I started towards my marker and both men started to wave their arms about. I thought 'How friendly', and waved back. Then they started running across the field towards me, shouting at me. 'Funny', I thought, but kept going – my eye fixed on my marker.

JIM. Stop, stop, what on earth do you think you are doing?

PEGGY. What's the matter, why do you want me to stop?

JIM. Where the hell are you going?

PEGGY. Cutting a new furrow...

JIM. Why don't you follow your marker?

PEGGY. But I am, there it is...

JIM. There's your marker – over there... You must need glasses.

PEGGY. I looked back and to my horror I had set a course of about forty-five degrees and had ploughed a lovely triangle shape.

JIM. You were doing so well… What went wrong?

PEGGY. Tears came into my eyes.

JIM. For goodness' sake, stop that and get down. I'll correct it for you this time, but be more careful in future.

PEGGY. He got on my tractor and I sat on the side mudguard. Jim drove quickly and expertly towards my marker, making a beautiful straight line for me to follow. After they'd gone – I put my glasses on to see if I could figure out where I'd gone wrong. What I'd thought was my marker was a pylon in the field across the other side of the river.

VERA. We took our tractor into Middleton on Saturday afternoons – me driving, Annie and Gracie sat one on each mudguard. We parked outside Woolworths and did the shopping. Ink – nine pence or one and three… better be nine pence.

POPPY. Tattoo lipstick – two and six…

VERA. Plus six pence purchase tax.

POPPY. Rose Dawn, Black Magic, Fire Red.

MARGIE. Fire Red?

PEGGY. Cadbury's ration bar.

MARGIE. 'Stockings in a bottle.'

VERA. Wright's Coal Tar Soap – one coupon.

MARGIE. Scrubbs Cloudy Ammonia.

PEGGY. Sanitary towels.

POPPY. Bicarbonate of soda.

PEGGY. Andrews Liver Salts.

VERA. Last night, Annie and I were dancing together in one of the barns. The farmer was standing in the doorway and then he said, 'I'll turn a blind eye since you're both good workers'... So we just carried on dancing.

From the radio, a BBC Home Service broadcast: Japan declares war/Pearl Harbour, 1941.

POPPY. The local vicar let me have a bath at the vicarage. We were only allowed one bath a week.

MARGIE. I was filthy dirty after a day's work. When there was a water shortage, the plug was taken from our bath so I stuffed a flannel in the plughole.

PEGGY. When there was a dance in the village, three of us would get in the bath together – standing up.

POPPY. Can't be modest.

VERA. Excellent chance for a sing-song.

They sing 'We are Land Girls'. To the tune of 'Oh, My Darling Clementine'.

> We are land girls, we are land girls,
> And we're proud to do our bit,
> Working, hoeing, reaping, sowing,
> Just to keep the nation fit.
> And our warden, what a warden,
> And her name I cannot tell,
> When she wakes us in the morning,
> How we wish she were in...

PEGGY. Heaven is the best place for our warden.

VERA. If there was a village dance, Annie and Grace spent the whole day working with their hair in curlers under a turban – no hairdressers.

POPPY. If we didn't have nylons, we painted brown seams down our legs with an eyebrow pencil or thick cocoa.

VERA. To get to some dances, Annie borrowed a tradesman's bike with a basket on the front. I would sit in the basket – because I never could cycle – and Annie would pedal us both to the village. If it was really cold, I wore my walking-out uniform, woollen socks and all. I was once asked to dance by a Scots sailor wearing a kilt – so there we were, me in the trousers… and him in a skirt!

POPPY. As we went into the hall, I noticed the rows of girls all waiting for partners as usual…

PEGGY. Oh, the 'Excuse Me Quicksteps'… the man asks the lady to dance – very polite –

SOLDIER (MARGIE). May I have this dance, please?

PEGGY. And then they'd say –

ANNOUNCER (POPPY). This is a lady's 'Excuse Me Quickstep'.

PEGGY. And if you hadn't been asked to dance, and you'd seen someone and thought, 'I quite like the look of him' – well, you'd go up to him, tap him on the shoulder and say, 'Excuse me, please' – and the lady would have to go and sit down and you'd have your partner.

POPPY. Suddenly there was a noise outside, of lorries and trucks and then crowds of American servicemen came in. They soon got talking to us and said they'd like to dance, did we mind?

ALL. Did we mind!

POPPY. It was wonderful.

PEGGY. The Americans would drive by us when we were working in the fields and would shout – 'Are you coming to the dance?' and we'd shout –

ALL. Yes!

POPPY. Chest to breast is better than breast to breast.

PEGGY. And they'd throw us Baby Ruth candy bars, Camel cigarettes, nylons and chewing gum. Oh, and at the dance they'd unravel a wad of notes. 'What would you like? A Pimm's No. 1?'

VERA. They were twelve and six a glass – as much as we
earned in a week.

Music begins.

PEGGY. Are you dancing?

POPPY. Are you asking?

PEGGY. Sure I'm asking!

POPPY. Then I'm dancing.

POPPY, PEGGY *and* VERA *dance to 'Chattanooga Choo
Choo'. Throughout this sequence, the focus changes from the
dancehall to* MARGIE *alone at her farm.*

MARGIE. I never got out. I'd be sitting in the dark kitchen –
there was no electricity – at a card table with no cloth on,
with me dinner just put on the green baize. And that was me
dinner, whatever it was; I couldn't see what I was eating.
Then I'd go to bed and listen to the wireless...

PEGGY. One man said to me, 'What would happen if I undid
those buttons?' I said 'You wouldn't see tomorrow!'

VERA. Undo my buttons? Not with dark-green bloomers
underneath.

POPPY. The commanding officers asked if we would like to
come to their camp.

PEGGY. Four hundred men and no dancing partners.

PEGGY, VERA *and* POPPY. Would we like hell!

POPPY. Transport to the camp twice a week, Tuesdays and
Thursdays.

MARGIE. Dried egg and a slice of bread... Oh, Pop, I'm
famishing...

PEGGY. Oh, but the food.

VERA. After living on rations, their food was out of this world:
trestle tables filled with stuff we hadn't seen for years – ice

cream of various flavours, huge bowls of tinned peaches, tinned meats, lumps of real butter –

VERA, POPPY *and* PEGGY. Oranges!

MARGIE. Some nights I'd write a letter home to me mam and pop. One time I sent them a dead rabbit as a treat. A few days later Mrs Bainbridge said to us –

MRS BAINBRIDGE. There's a parcel for you, but it smells so bad I've left it outside.

MARGIE. It was the rabbit, I'd addressed it to meself.

PEGGY. They played all the popular music: Ink Spots, Duke Ellington, Glen Miller.

POPPY. There was a French-Canadian airman smoking black Sobranies.

PEGGY. 'Whispering Grass', 'Do Nothing Till You Hear from Me'.

VERA. 'Take the A-Train', 'Tuxedo Junction'.

PEGGY. 'Sky Lark', 'Chattanooga', 'Kalamazoo' and the 'Moonlight Serenade'… I was wearing my one and only dress – a pretty turquoise colour and very suitable for dancing. Flight Lieutenant Martin Maine and I returned a little late, around eleven o'clock – and as the vicarage gates were locked at ten o'clock, this presented a small problem… as the gates were approximately six feet high. My tall Canadian escort…

POPPY. Canadians are the best.

PEGGY.…lifted me up, to stand me on his shoulders, so I could climb onto the gate. It was quite a long jump down on the other side, but we were a fairly athletic lot of lasses. As I jumped, my treasured dress caught at the back and ripped all the way from the hem to the neck! I had to take off my dress, turn it around and hold it together at the front. Martin almost collapsed with laughter.

VERA. We were driven to a dance by a very grumpy English soldier. He quarrelled with his girlfriend, and at the end of

the dance, we found he'd left without us. Well, I'd had quite
a few port and lemons by this time, and decided that it would
be perfectly reasonable to 'acquire' a lorry. I drove us all the
way home, no lights or anything, but what with being a bit
tipsy, I couldn't quite negotiate the gateposts at the bottom of
the farm track, so I parked the lolleree, I parked the rolly... I
parked. And we walked the rest of the way back to the farm.

VERA, POPPY *and* PEGGY *sing 'Would You Like to Swing
on a Star' by Jimmy Van Heusen and Johnny Burke.*

When I got up in the morning to go and return the lorry, it
was gone.

POPPY. Friends signed us in if we were a little late home.
Twenty-five-mile bicycle ride, climb in through the down-
stairs window, bed.

PEGGY. I was returning home late one evening from a
dance... again... and was walking past Mr Clare's farm
when I heard this awful groaning coming from the
shippon. I looked in and saw that one of the cows was
trying to give birth, she was in some difficulty and seemed
to be exhausted. I could see the hooves of the calf and
having seen how the cowmen had helped in this situation, I
tied one end of a rope around the hooves and the other end
to the gate. Each time the cow contracted, I heaved with
all my might on the gate. Eventually, the nose appeared
and he soon slithered out onto the waiting bed of straw!
What a relief! And what a miraculous sight. The calf was
black and had white eyes – so I christened him Panda. He
was soon up on shaky legs, sucking the first flow of milk
from his mum. I felt quite chuffed with myself having
gone through that experience on my own and I got a pat on
the back from Mr Clare.

VERA. Four thirty a.m. woken up by the noise of the generator,
which lights the cowshed and hammering on our bedroom
window –

VOICE (MARGIE). Wakey, wakey.

VERA. My alarm call for two years. Then the smell of the byre, the cows, the rattle of chains being fastened around each neck, the steamy straw, the hay and cake being fed to the impatient beasts, swishing tails, the occasional cough – Daisy, Firefly, Buttercup, Pansy, some mornings I fell asleep on the job.

MARGIE. Early morning, on me bike, I saw boxes of ammunition, rifles and other war necessities hidden underneath the hedges along the lanes – mile after mile of them.

POPPY. We were working in a turnip field, the droning of these aeroplanes kept going – normally you hear a plane and it disappears but it didn't, it went on. We looked up, the sky was black with planes, they were just circling round – all gathering, obviously to go on a bombing raid.

VERA. Cutting fodder for the animals, the new girl Phyllis was so small we lost her in a field of kale.

PEGGY. Most of the jokes we heard, the soldiers would bring home. Someone would hear it and come back to the hostel and tell us and we'd all laugh. The ones we did hear, we knew so well we'd number them and when cutting brussel sprouts in the field – well, it'd be quiet, the mail had been, someone had died, a bomb, everything would be quiet and people would be thinking and then someone would call out 'Five!', 'Three!', 'Seven!' – we only generally had up to seven jokes. And there would be a pause and people would think of that joke, and then we'd all burst out laughing.

MARGIE. Me mam said her friend, Mrs Goodbody, was taking a bath when the siren went. A bomb fell and she was shot out into the road still in the bath – she wasn't injured – except for her pride!

VERA. The bottle-washing machine packed in. By seven o'clock we were faced with one hundred and fifty dirty milk bottles. I had some sherry I'd won in a raffle so Annie introduced Isla, the new girl, to the demon drink. Isla, Annie and I drank heavy, sweet sherry – from the best half-pint milk bottles on the market and the work went with a swing and a song, but by the time we were packing the steriliser, Isla was starting to swing and sway, so we sent her back to the cottage. By the time we came in, she was staring at the black wind-up gramophone in a very puzzled way as the turntable wouldn't revolve. Annie had to point out that she had her elbow leaning on it.

Song – 'White Cliffs of Dover' by Walter Kent and Nat Burton.

Perhaps the radio is playing softly now.

POPPY (*reading*). 'You want me to tell you that I love you. Words are limited. Suppose I say… (*Under breath during the following dialogue.*) that absolute and unquestioning love is a chord of many notes – and at present I have not all the notes, as I do not know all you, but I have a few notes which sound very sweet – I have enough notes to make a harmony.'

PEGGY. During blackouts, we'd lie around on our bunk beds.

VERA. Annie had this cocoa tin – we cut a hole in the lid, fixed it under the bulb.

POPPY (*reading*). 'As I do not know all you, but I have a few notes.'

MARGIE. I'd knit.

VERA. Game of crib.

PEGGY. Rose would murder a record of 'The Lights are Going Out All Over Europe'.

POPPY (*reading*). 'To make a harmony.'

PEGGY. We'd talk about the boys, write letters – until the siren went.

LAND GIRLS *respond to the sound of the siren,* PEGGY *reaches out to turn the light off.*

Blackout.

End of Act One.

ACT TWO

1942–1946

From the radio, a BBC Home Service broadcast: Sir Winston Churchill's speech '…some chicken, some neck…'. The GIRLS *gather together to perform 'Old Gang Labour'. The following lines may be divided among the* LAND GIRLS *in a different order.*

PEGGY. The Heydi Heidi Hoes present…

ALL. 'Old Gang Labour'.

VERA. The gallant House of Commons,
    Sought the harvest field one day,
    And they set about the problem,
    In a parliamentary way –
    Calling first on Herbert Morrison,
    A system to devise –
    So he set up ten Commons Committees,
    And sat down to supervise.

PEGGY. They discoursed with dash and vigour,
    On the job they meant to do,
    And the plans they had for afterwards,
    When all the work was through.
    Then they called on Ernie Bevin,
    For a speech of pep and punch –
    And he stressed the need for leadership –
    And led 'em off for lunch.

POPPY. Then they came back to their labours,
    And they sat down with a sigh,
    And Sir Kingsley Wood said cautiously –
    And doubt was in his eye –
    'Now I really have a strong desire,

> To do the job today –
> But suppose we get it finished,
> And the farmer cannot pay?'

MARGIE. So they all went back to London,
> Where they talked of sacrifice,
> And reminded us that victory,
> Was bound to have its price;
> And they railed at absenteeism,
> And said it was a sin –
> And...

ALL. A couple o' little Land Girls
> Went and got the harvest in.

MARGIE. The supervisor from the WLA came out to see how I was doing. Her name was Mrs Bottomly.

MRS BOTTOMLY (POPPY). Margorie, do you ever go out?

MARGIE. No.

MRS BOTTOMLY. Do you get paid?

MARGIE. No.

MRS BOTTOMLY. Why not?

MARGIE. I don't know. So she got onto Mr Bainbridge and he just turns round and he says –

MR BAINBRIDGE. Well – it's like this, missus. You send all these kids out to us. You expect us to feed 'em, bed 'em and board 'em for nowt and then you want us to pay 'em as well. No, she gets enough out of us.

MARGIE. So he was blacklisted and I was moved to Bankside Farm in Kildale. To get there I kept going up and up into the fells – and I remember thinking to meself, 'If we go any higher, we won't be far off heaven.'

POPPY. I wanted him to take me to the Winter Ball in East Lothian, I had to get Saturday morning off, so I said that my grandfather – who was ninety-six – was dying and I would like to see him before he did. Took the Friday-night train, sitting up, of course. When I saw him I said, 'Grandfather, I am going to a ball at Gosforth tonight, and in order to get the time off I said you were dying.'

GRANDFATHER. Yes, my dear, I am.

POPPY. We went to the ball, two nights on the train... but it was worth it.

PEGGY. Jim and I had been to the pictures, and of course I needed my glasses in order to see the picture clearly. But by then I was able to say to myself, 'What the heck, he has to know some time,' so I just took them out of my bag and put them on.

JIM. They suit you –

PEGGY. Was all he said. On the way home I told him the story I've just told you about ploughing and he said –

JIM. Yes, we knew, we had a good laugh about it.

PEGGY. You see, they'd seen me take my glasses off and put them in my pocket.

JIM. After all, we're not short-sighted, you know!

VERA. Library night and new books, it looked a good lot. I chose *Hogbend's Mathematics for the Million* – I thought, that will keep me quiet for weeks.

MARGIE. On me arrival at Bankside Farm, the first thing I noticed was an open copy of the *Christian Herald* on the kitchen table, and one of the first questions the lady farmer asked was –

LADY FARMER. Do you go to chapel?

MARGIE. Yes, and we take the *Christian Herald* at home. That seemed to clinch it. After a cup of tea, I went to the toilet. The toilet had a chain – I was heady with relief. There was no toilet paper, but there in a little wooden box at the side of the toilet was an old Methodist hymn book. I did think it was

taking things a bit far, *Christian Herald* on the kitchen table
and Methodist hymn book in the toilet! She'd reached the
Christmas carols when I arrived, number 130 – 'It Came
Upon a Midnight Clear'.

VERA. Annie and I started journals. I called mine 'Diary of the
Red Armlet: Thoughts and Reflections'. Annie called hers…

ANNIE (MARGIE). 'Shovelling Shit'.

She reads her own diary.

VERA. 'November 6th: swede-bashing again. November 7th:
the doctor says Annie's red sores are ringworm and is
sending her home to get better. November 8th: prisoners of
war arrived to work on the farm, Germans have yellow
circles on their backs and Italians have blue.'

MARGIE. Cycling up the lane at seven o'clock in the morning,
I could hear a lovely tenor voice wafting across the fields.

POPPY. We were meant to be kept apart, but I managed to share
cigarettes with one of them and he gave me a St Christopher
badge on a circle of red wool.

PEGGY. The Italians were a friendly talkative lot –

ITALIAN (POPPY). *Buon giorno, signorina, sei libera di
venire con me, bella, bella…* You very beautiful today!

PEGGY. – and if they could help you down from your tractor, it
was the highlight of their day.

ITALIAN. *Bellissima.*

PEGGY. They weren't particularly good workers and would
slide down into a ditch and have a sleep. Some of them
drank Andrews Liver Salts as a refreshment. At lunchtimes
we'd teach them how to knit and they made us rings out of
tuppenny pieces – amazing!

VERA. The Germans weren't Nazis, just ordinary people. We
took them presents of chocolate from our rations. One of them
carved me a beautiful model of two horses out of oak, smooth

and polished. We had letters from them too. I couldn't bring myself to burn them, so I put them in a tin and buried them.

POPPY. If it rained we all went inside to mend sacks, but if it snowed we carried on working outside and the POWs went in. White bread for them –

PEGGY. Black bread for us.

VERA. Annie wrote that she wasn't coming back. She said she'd shovelled enough shite to last a lifetime – she was going to stay at home for Christmas and then apply to join the new Timber Corps.

POPPY. Cutting holly to decorate the farm, there was an atmosphere… that particular stillness that comes with the fall of snow. I felt we were on a soundless moon. No sweet song of birds, no lowing of cattle or bleating of sheep, no rustle of wind, no human footstep, all was white, unending; the only blaze of colour was the remains of a setting sun.

PEGGY. A farmer's son fetched a toboggan he had made. Six of us scrambled onto it and – whizz – down the hill we speeded! We really flew down at a terrific speed! The wind whistled by us and we'd catch the low-hanging boughs of the trees, and as we passed under them we'd be showered with a host of powdered jewels. We always had to jump clear of the sledge before the final crash! Well, there was a wall at the bottom and unless you wanted to decorate it, you had to jump!

VERA. At five-thirty on the Friday before Christmas, there was still some of the rick to thresh. We really hoped we wouldn't be expected to stay on until it was finished. But the farmer signed our timesheets and let us go. As we were cycling out of the farmyard he called us back but we pretended not to hear him. As I was the worst cyclist, last through the gate – the farmer caught up with me.

FARMER. Here, take this to the Post Office.

VERA. In the road outside everyone crowded round, and there, written on the inside of a cigarette packet it read –

A LAND GIRL. Pay the bearers five shillings each.

GIRLS. 'The bearers'? That's us!

VERA. Five shillings!

*From the radio, a BBC Home Service broadcast: Air Chief
Marshall, Sir Arthur Harris, on bombing Germany, 1943.*

POPPY. Four thirty in the morning and the night was alive with
stars. The silence was tangible as I wended my way by
bicycle to keep a tryst. It was his birthday.

PEGGY. We stopped working about four o'clock for a drink and
a snack. The moon rose behind a line of fan-shaped elms,
then someone started to sing 'Silent Night', from a group of
Italians came their rich tenor voices, then strong German
voices singing 'Stille Nacht' and our sopranos, each singing
in our own language. We stood together in feelings of
longing for home, family, and no more war. For five minutes
or more, voices rose and mingled and we were at peace.
Then it was time to leave – with much waving of hands,
farewells of 'Gute Nacht', 'Buonanotte' and 'Goodnight', we
returned to our hostel, and the men to their camps.

The GIRLS *sing 'Silent Night' together, with all the
languages blending.*

(*English:*)

>Silent night, Holy night,
>All is calm, all is bright,
>Round yon virgin mother and child,
>Holy infant so tender and mild,
>Sleep in heavenly peace,
>Sleep in heavenly peace.

(*German:*)

>Stille Nacht, heilige Nacht,
>Alles schläft, einsam wacht
>nur das traute hochheilige Paar
>holder Knabe in lockigem Haar
>Schlaf in himmlischer Ruh,
>Schlaf in himmlischer Ruh.

(*Italian:*)

> Astro del ciel, Pargol divin
> Mite agnello, Redentor,
> Tu che i vati da lungi sognar,
> Tu che angeliche voci nunziar,
> Luce dona alle menti,
> Pace infondi nei cuori.

VERA. Culford St Mary Forestry Camp, January 28th – it's from Annie!

(*Reading.*) Dear Vera,

You wrote saying, how is the Timber Corps, well the hours are different, finished by five, sometimes as early as three depending on the weather; and no shovelling sh…!

We live twelve to a hut, ours is number four, and sleep in bunk beds. This has proved very dangerous for yours truly, as I sleep below Myra, who insists on keeping mothballs under her pillow, one of which fell out and landed in my mouth last week.

Tools of my new trade are: a billy hook, a sickle…

VERA *continues to read silently.*

ANNIE….a billy hook, a sickle and a really heavy penknife – better than yours. We are marched up to the forest area every morning, and I now know how to use a cross-cut saw, and how to put a 'fall' in a pine tree – see diagram.

Actually I'm a bit proud of myself, because I've been promoted to pit-prop measurer, at a wage of thirteen six a week, don't you know! We load the props onto the lorry, and take them to the station, riding on top. The smell of the resin is delicious, but the singing is appalling. The other job we have had is to slice up elm trees for coffins.

We're near to Coltishall Airfield, a fighter-pilot base, so you can guess what the dances are like. The pilots ask us for dates galore – but not for long. They are brave.

So, not bad, eh? What with ending the day with a...

VERA (*resumes reading the letter*). What with ending the day with a mug of cocoa. Give my regards to Isla and Grace and Scarlett O'Hara the red heifer.

ANNIE. Miss you –

VERA. Annie.

MARGIE. The farmer says to us –

FARMER. There's a cow there. It wants servicing. Take her out, down t'lane, and there'll be a man waiting for you at bottom.

MARGIE. Well, on the other side of the lane was the glider factory, where all the workers were making planes. It was all hush-hush. And it happened to be that it was their dinner break and they were all coming out. So I've got Bessy with a halter on and we're strolling along the lane, me in me little uniform. And as I went past all the workers were shouting –

GLIDER-FACTORY MEN (VERA, POPPY, PEGGY). Way-hey! We know where you're going.

MARGIE. And everybody was whistling –

PEGGY *whistles*.

And calling to me...

GLIDER-FACTORY MAN (VERA). Mary had a little lamb...

MARGIE. But I had a cow. So I got to the bottom of the lane and the man was there –

SERVICE FARMER. Right, take her in there, into the arena, and keep hold of the rope. I shan't be a minute.

MARGIE. So I'm holding on to Bessy and all these fellas are stood round. The next thing I hear is a great big corrugated gate being pulled aside then this 'SNIFF SNIFF SNIIFFF'. And this big thing come trotting in like this and he gets behind Bessy. Oh well, I nearly died. He upped on top of her and I'm looking up at him and I went, 'OOH MAM!'

SERVICE FARMER. Hush – you'll spoil job.

MARGIE. I'd never seen owt like it in me life. When the bull
    had finished the farmer took him out, then he come back to
    me and he says –

SERVICE FARMER. There thou is, you can tek her home now.
    See if job's done. By the way, are you courting?

MARGIE. I said, 'No, why?'

SERVICE FARMER. Well, that's what married life's all about.

    PEGGY *and* POPPY *perform* – *'Straight from the Cow's
    Mouth'.*

POPPY. Comments on Artificial Insemination –

PEGGY. Straight from the Cow's Mouth.

PEGGY. I have just given birth to a calf, sir,
    And with motherly pride I am full.

POPPY. But please do not laugh, pray do not chaff,
    When I tell you I've not had a bull.

PEGGY. The farmyard's the dreariest place, sir,
    The meadow is no longer gay.

POPPY. Since the one spot of fun,
    In the year's dismal run,
    Has by science been taken away.

PEGGY. No bull has embraced me with passion.

POPPY. I've not had the ghost of a binge,
    I've never been loved –

PEGGY. – But ruthlessly shoved,
    By a dirty great brass-bound syringe.

POPPY. You may think this is all very well, sir,
    And there are some things a cow cannot say,

PEGGY. But those Land Army tarts,
    Who play with my parts,
    Still get it –

PEGGY *and* POPPY. – the old-fashioned way.

POPPY. The new Foreman introduced himself to me when I was hoeing turnips on my own.

FOREMAN. We'll be seeing a lot of each other, I know a lot about you Land Girls and what you get up to.

POPPY. From then on I never knew a moment's peace. He would jump out from behind the barn door or somewhere else and grab me. His favourite saying was –

FOREMAN. Give me a feel, till the baker's been…

PEGGY. Sometimes you have to be a fast runner.

VERA. I was fetching water from the pump to brew some tea. One of the Italian chaps was sitting on the steps and asked me what I was doing. Then he started to cry, he said he missed his family – 'I miss Mama, Papa and bambinos.' 'Oh dear, don't cry, the war will be over soon and then you'll be able to go home and be with your mama and bambinos. I'm sorry, I have to go and get the water, they'll be wondering where I am.' And when I turned round, he had disappeared.

But when I came back through the archway, he jumped out at me, grabbed me round the waist and pushed me against the wall. I'm holding this pan of water and I said, 'Get off! Leave me alone, get off.' He kept pressing me hard up against the archway, against the brickwork of the archway. 'You're hurting my back, get off, you horrible man.' He still didn't – so I don't know where I got the strength, I lifted up this big pan of water, and threw it over him, he was absolutely soaked, and he swore at me. When I got back they all said –

ALL. Where's the water?

VERA. If you want water, you go and get it.

PEGGY. Just –

POPPY. My prongs stuck into his stave just a few inches from his face… I was shouting and swearing… 'Leave me alone or the next time I'll kill you.'

PEGGY. Sometimes you have to be a fast runner.

MARGIE. Dolly, a friend of mine, was miles out, working for this old couple, and she was petrified of the old farmer because he was abusing her. Every time she went into the barn he followed her and abused her. When she went to bed, she'd sit there with all her clothes on. She never got undressed. She'd put the bolt on, cos he used to come and try the door every night. She could see the latch moving up and down and she daren't tell anybody. I said, 'Why not?' She said, 'Who would have believed me?'

The GIRLS *sing 'When this Lousy War is Over'*

> When this lousy war is over, no more Land Army for me,
> When I get my civvie clothes on, oh how happy I shall be.
> No more digging up potatoes, no more threshing out the corn.
> We will make that bossy foreman, regret the day that he was born.

From the radio, a BBC Home Service broadcast: the bombing of Nuremburg or Sir Winston Churchill's speech, 1944.

Rounding up cows on a dark, foggy March morning and encouraging them to move with a stick, only to find I was trying to move a bush.

POPPY. Disking and harrowing…

VERA. Working with the horses…

POPPY. Till the clods of earth were broken down into fine-textured soil ready for seeds to be sown.

MARGIE. Hoeing.

PEGGY. The Foreman told us not to straighten our backs – we didn't realise he was being kind to us – if you keep down and keep working it stops you getting backache.

MARGIE. I walked miles, planting and sowing.

PEGGY, POPPY *and* VERA. Hailstones.

PEGGY. Mud-encrusted eyes, nose, lips.

POPPY. March winds that blew dust in our eyes.

MARGIE. Primroses under the hedge, Easter –

She starts to sing 'There is a Green Hill Far Away'.

PEGGY. Dawn choruses –

VERA. Lambing –

POPPY. When he came back from ops we walked out together in the sunshine.

VERA. I loved the names of the fields: Red Brinks, Underling Meadow, Greyfields.

POPPY. Lapwing's eggs lying open to the world in a drill.

VERA. I took the *Farmers Weekly*. I got strong. I lambed eighty-eight ewes in three weeks that spring, night and day, day and night, sitting in the dark listening for the grunts of the ewes. I salted pig.

PEGGY. Dear Mum, are you still alive?

POPPY. Mummy and Daddy were having coffee with some friends in the lounge one evening. A bomb knocked down half the house. My family were smothered in plaster and very shocked. I was allowed to go home on compassionate leave.

PEGGY. You heard from Henry yet? I bet he's giving 'em hell.

POPPY. I found my cat, Crock, sitting by the bombed remains of the house, wonderful to find him without apparent injury. Fortunately we had Grandpa's house left to us in Selly Oak. I scooped up pussy and buttoned him up under my mac and was getting on the tram to Selly Oak and a man said, 'Dear, if you're pregnant, have my seat.' When I explained what it was, all the ladies on the tram made a great fuss of him.

PEGGY. Last week we were lambing and you never guess what I did.

POPPY. Our family arrived at Wedley Park Road to start a new life. I went back to the WLA.

PEGGY. Jim said you couldn't see me for dust.

VERA. I was moved. Down to a farm near Arundel. Thirty boisterous bullocks, mainly Friesian and Hereford Cross.

PEGGY. Least the light lasts longer.

MARGIE. I was sent to a rest home in Torquay for two weeks. It was a massive house, the Americans had donated it to the WLA who, they said, were doing –

AMERICAN. A damned mighty-fine job.

MARGIE. The landing was all polished, the staircase was like something out of *Gone With the Wind*. I was so busy looking at the paintings on the ceiling, I missed my footing on the top stair and went careering down, swerved round the bend and landed at the bottom. This sergeant-major-type Matron appeared. I said, 'Hello.'

MATRON. Get up. What are you doing down there? I don't allow this sort of behaviour.

MARGIE. I slipped, miss… But she never spoke to me again. It was run like a parlour for debutantes instead of a rest home for us muck-pluggers. But we're all in the same Army… Why try to be something you're not?

PEGGY. PS, let me know about my dress material as soon as you can… you never know! Peg.

VERA. I was standing in the doorway of the farmhouse and I saw this great black doodlebug coming straight towards the house, I mean it was coming straight towards me. I thought, what shall I do? Shall I run? What should I do? Then one of the doodlebug wings clipped a tree – the house was surrounded by trees and the whole thing tipped sideways and came down in the next field. I was blown off my feet, my shoes were blown across the room. No one was hurt. The whole village came up to the farm, certain we'd had a direct hit. Next day working in the fields, I realised I would never hear the noise of a doodlebug over the tractor engine.

MARGIE. By the time I got back to Bankside Farm, the chicken-sexers had arrived. It used to be done by trained Japanese men, but just before Pearl Harbour, they all disappeared like snow in summer.

POPPY. V1s were really scary. After the engine stopped there was a sudden silence and you held your breath – till the explosion came. I sang to myself in the ditches. 'Dido's Lament', 'When I Am Laid in Earth', and 'Have Mercy Lord On Me'.

PEGGY. We were having an exhausting day – hoeing what seemed to be a concrete path. It was really warm, so we took off our shirts. We saw a lone plane coming towards us. Then it began to dive lower, so we thought it was some cheeky Air Force man coming to get a closer look. It was a stray German plane returning home and he decided to empty his machine gun on us. I don't think I've ever run so fast.

VERA. The Army started coming through.

PEGGY. British, American.

POPPY. Canadians.

MARGIE. Every road in the area was filled with armoured tanks, vehicles –

PEGGY. Men.

ALL. Leaving.

PEGGY. Then one morning the rush was over.

POPPY. The invasion had started.

VERA. I worked with a man who said he was a teacher. He said to me –

CONSCIENTIOUS OBJECTOR. I don't know what I'm going to do at the end of the war because, you know, will we ever get our jobs back?

VERA. After the first war they didn't. They wouldn't employ them if they'd been conscientious objectors.

PEGGY. I met a lot of COs – some were stretcher-bearers in the First World War – must have been a terrible job. They weren't cowards at all. But they were hated.

POPPY. An American single-pilot fighter plane came down in a field. It crash-landed limping home from a bombing raid. A local girl rushed across the field to help get the pilot out, but before she could do so the petrol ignited, the plane caught fire and exploded, killing the pilot and the girl. I thought of our Lord's words: Greater love hath no man than this, that a man… that a woman, lay down her life for her friend.

MARGIE. Dolly got married to an air gunner and she told us that when he came home on leave and they were together, he used to wake up screaming in the night.

They sing quietly, 'If You Want to Go to Heaven.' To the tune of 'She'll Be Coming Round the Mountain.'

If you want to go to Heaven when you die,
You must wear a green pullover and a tie,
And a little khaki bonnet,
With WLA on it,
If you want to go to Heaven when you die.

You have to be there to know.

Reprise of 'If You Want to Go to Heaven.' From the radio, a BBC Home Service broadcast: Declaration of D-Day, 1944.

POPPY. On May 7th, Victory in Europe was assured!

VERA. Oh God, I'll have to go home.

MARGIE. And everyone went –

ALL. Wild!

POPPY. The Italians danced around giving everyone a hug and a kiss.

ITALIANS (PEGGY, POPPY *and* MARGIE). We go home soon! *Andiamo a casa!*

POPPY. Old George, said –

OLD GEORGE. No more work today!

POPPY. He went home and came back with a large flagon of cider.

VERA. On VE night I cycled into Arundel and helped burn the furniture from the Royal Norfolk Hotel on a huge bonfire…

PEGGY. Burning tar barrels rolled down Castle Hill.

VERA. Chichester Cathedral was illuminated.

ALL. Fireworks!

MARGIE. We were out with the milk float when we heard, so we decorated Polly Pony and the milk cart with orange blossom pinched from someone's back garden.

POPPY. In our village there was a fancy-dress parade. Joyce persuaded me to go as 'A Land Girl's Gratuity':

ALL. One overcoat, one pair of socks, one pair of shoes –

POPPY. That's all!

VERA. That's all we're getting?

POPPY. This I wore – with the addition of a swimsuit – and was awarded second prize!

All applaud.

Two shillings presented to me by the local vicar who said –

VICAR. I thought you were very good.

VERA. The war isn't over, the boys are still in Burma.

PEGGY. I got engaged to Jim, it was my twentieth birthday. Next day it was –

They sing 'Back to the Land' by E.K. Loring, P. Adkins and J. Moncrieff.

Singing can continue quietly under the following dialogue.

POPPY. By the end of May our outward appearance changed considerably.

PEGGY. My hair went the colour of straw and felt like it.

MARGIE. Sometimes we wore our swimsuits.

VERA. Our blood became quite black.

POPPY. We saw quite a lot of it, as we frequently hacked ourselves with billhooks or stuck forks through our feet.

PEGGY. There was a training airfield nearby and the pilots came to our local pub. One evening the conversation turned to the subject of –

PILOT. How do you spend a penny when you're often so far from habitation?

PEGGY. We said behind a hedge or a tree. A few days later we were working near the airfield when we saw this Tiger Moth plane fly over, and from it we saw something fall into the next field. Me and Rose went across to where the object had landed – it was a toilet roll.

ALL. Harvesting.

VERA. We worked from five o'clock in the morning milking to ten o'clock at night harvesting.

PEGGY. It never seemed to grow dark. Double summertime.

POPPY. The local farmer asked if he could borrow me at harvest time, in exchange for a cartload of manure.

MARGIE. When we were getting in a late hay or corn harvest, we started at five thirty with a cup of tea in the kitchen, which we drank out of our saucers, because it was quicker.

POPPY. Twenty-six acres when harvest was in full flow. Sheaves were passed up to me from a cart, I had to catch them on my pitchfork and pass them back to the men behind me – I felt like the girl on the Ovaltine advertisement.

VERA. That evening we ate tomatoes, ripened in Old Bert's tin helmet.

PEGGY. We rolled up or cut off our dungarees –

MARGIE. A dreadful crime – if spotted.

PEGGY. The general opinion being held was that Land Girls
    wore too much in winter –

ALL. – too little in summer.

VERA (*takes out a letter*). In the middle of harvest, I got a letter
    from Annie's mother to say that Annie was driving a Bedford
    truck, distributing wooden fencing posts to various sites, and
    on her way back to base she had to stop at a railway crossing
    as the gates were closed. Somehow the handbrake was not
    applied, her foot slipped onto the accelerator and the truck
    went through the gate straight into an oncoming express
    train. The girls in the back got away with cuts and bruises.
    Annie and the Foreman were killed instantly.

MARGIE. Those long summer days – I don't know how we
    survived working all day in the fields in the heat. As the sun
    got high, me face got sunburnt, seeds went down my neck,
    the pitchfork blistered my hands. But I thought, I didn't
    make bullets, I grew food. And when I went to bed at night, I
    started to pray for strength, but I fell asleep before I could
    finish.

PEGGY. The grain was in and it was time for half a shandy at
    the local. I put my hand in one of the sacks and pulled out a
    single grain and I looked at it and thought – I grew that.

MARGIE. Pauline and I were sorting potatoes from the clamp
    where they'd been stored since the previous autumn, when
    we heard the Japanese had surrendered. The smell of rotting
    potatoes always reminds me of that day.

POPPY. When he was going over on ops, he'd say, 'I'll fly over,
    I'll go low, so you'll know it's me,' and that's what he did.
    And every time he came back, it didn't matter what time of
    night it was, midnight, one o'clock, he would telephone just
    to say he was back safely. One day he was reported missing
    on camp, I said, 'I don't think so…' Then the telephone
    didn't ring… there was no swooping plane… Then I knew.

PEGGY. I married Jim, we were able to have the church bells
    rung at our wedding. It was the first time they'd been rung in

peace since 1939. It seemed as if the whole world was rejoicing... just for me.

The LAND GIRLS *split the lines of the poem 'Harvest Home' by Enid Barraud between them.*

January 1965. The four WOMEN *are standing in the crowd watching the funeral cortege of Churchill pass by. Muffled bells from St Paul's Cathedral. The gun carriage passes... They watch and absorb the scene in silence, partly still back in the world they have just recreated. Gun salute and the Air Force fly past. They look up. There is a lark singing above.*

During the following dialogue they become aware of each other – and their shared experience in the Women's Land Army.

MARGIE. You had to be there to know.

POPPY. We lived it.

VERA. The Forgotten Army?

PEGGY. I'd do it all again.

The End.